HIGH HOLIDAYS & MORE

An Interactive Guide for Kids

Rosh Hashanah, Yom Kippur
Sukkot, Shmini Atzeret/Simchat Torah

SARAH MAZOR
ILLUSTRATIONS BY MAZORBOOKS

AUTHOR'S NOTE

Thank you for purchasing *High Holidays & More: An Interactive Guide for Kids.*

During *Tishrei*, the first month of the Jewish Calendar, Jews celebrate four holidays: *Rosh Hashanah, Yom Kippur, Sukkot, and Shmini Atzeret/Simchat Torah,* each with its unique rituals, customs, and meaning.

In this enjoyable interactive book, you will find,
- An overview of each of the holidays
- Highlights of unique holiday characteristics
- Description of important customs and traditions

The age-appropriate texts and explanations and the lovely images that can be colored in, entertain and educate.

BONUS: Look for additional information about rituals and observances at the end of the book.

Happy and sweet New Year!
Sarah Mazor

HAPPY HOLIDAYS

חַג שָׂמֵחַ

The Hebrew Calendar

לוּחַ הַשָּׁנָה הָעִבְרִי

Ha-lu-ach Ha-Iv-ri

The twelve months of the Jewish calendar begin
with the month of Tishrei and end with Elul.
Be sure to follow the cycle counterclockwise,
just as you would read Hebrew: Right to left.

The Hebrew Calendar
לוּחַ הַשָּׁנָה הָעִבְרִי
Ha-lu-ach Ha-Iv-ri

תִּשְׁרֵי	נִיסָן
חֶשְׁוָן	אִיָּר
כִּסְלֵו	סִיוָן
טֵבֵת	תַּמּוּז
שְׁבָט	אָב
אֲדָר	אֱלוּל

Jewish Holidays During the Month of Tishrei

חַגֵי תִּשְׁרֵי

Cha-gei Tish-rei

The Jewish new year begins
with *Tishrei*, the first month of the
Jewish calendar.
The year opens with the celebration
and observance of holidays that
inspire us to look forward and
strive for better tomorrows.

Jewish holidays that fall during *Tishrei*:
Rosh Hashanah, Yom Kippur, Sukkot,
and *Shmini Atzeret/Simchat Torah.*

כְּתִיבָה

וַחֲתִימָה

טוֹבָה

Rosh Hashanah Greetings

Chag sa-me-ach (חג שמח) - happy holiday, is the usual Jewish holiday greeting. But for *Rosh Hashanah*, there are additional, special greetings. *K'tiva v'chatima tova* (כתיבה וחתימה טובה) and *L'shana tova tikatevu v'techatemu* (לשנה טובה תכתבו ותחתמו) are two ways of wishing one another a good inscription and sealing [in the book of life]. *L'shana tova* (לשנה טובה), *a* shortened version, is often used outside of Israel. In Israel, the usual greeting is *Shana tova* (שנה טובה) - good year, or *Shana tova u'metuka* (שנה טובה ומתוקה) - good and sweet year.

פְּתִיבָה

וַחֲתִימָה

טוֹבָה

Rosh Hashanah Cards

פַּרְטִיסֵי בְּרָכָה לְרֹאשׁ הַשָּׁנָה

Kar-ti-sei Bra-cha Le-Rosh Hashanah

*It is customary to send friends and family
Rosh Hashanah cards wishing all a sweet new year*

HAPPY HOLIDAYS

חַג שָׂמֵחַ

Rosh Hashanah

HAPPY HOLIDAYS

חַג שָׂמֵחַ

Rosh Hashanah
רֹאשׁ הַשָּׁנָה

Rosh Hashanah, which means 'head of the year', is a two-day holiday that is celebrated on the first and second days of the month of *Tishrei*.

Rosh Hashanah is also known by four additional names. Each of the names describes a unique characteristic of the holiday.
Yom Teruah - Day of Blowing the *Shofar*,
Yom Hazikaron - Day of Remembrance,
Yom Hadin - Day of Judgement, and
Yom Harat Olam - the world's birthday.

Day of Shofar Blowing
יוֹם תְּרוּעָה

Yom Te-ru-ah

The name Yom Teruah (יום תרועה) refers to the obligation of hearing shofar blowing during the Rosh Hashanah day services at the synagogue.

HAPPY HOLIDAYS

חַג שָׂמֵחַ

DAY OF REMEMBRANCE
יוֹם הַזִּכָּרוֹן

Yom Ha-zi-ka-ron

Kindness

The name Yom Hazikaron (יום הזכרון) is how
Rosh Hashanah is referred to in the Talmud.
On this day, God recalls the deeds and behaviors
of each and every one of His creations.

HAPPY HOLIDAYS

חַג שָׂמֵחַ

Day of Judgement
יוֹם הַדִּין

Yom Ha-din

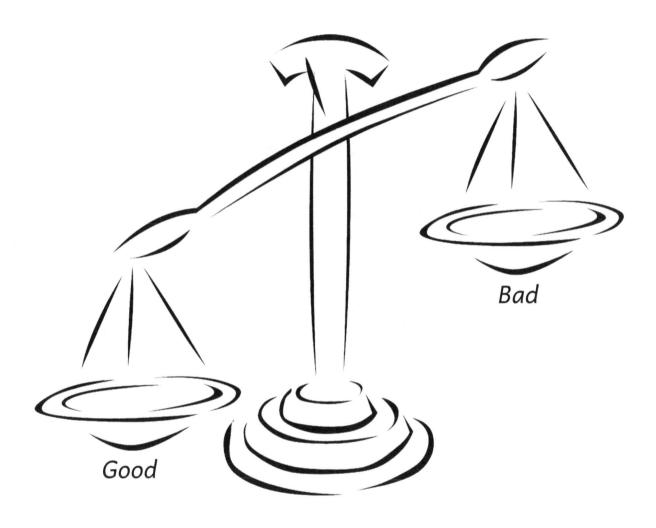

Good

Bad

Yom Hadin (יום הדין) is another one of the holiday's names. On Rosh Hashanah, God judges all human beings and weighs their good deeds against their bad ones.

HAPPY HOLIDAYS

חַג שָׂמֵחַ

THE WORLD'S BIRTHDAY
הַיוֹם הֲרַת עוֹלָם

Ha-yom Ha-rat O-lam

Rosh Hashanah is also called Yom Harat Olam
(יום הרת עולם) – today is the birthday of the world.
On this day, God created Adam and Eve.

HAPPY HOLIDAYS

חַג שָׂמֵחַ

RITUALS & CUSTOMS

טְקָסִים וּמִנְהָגִים

T'ka-sim U'min-ha-gim

Many of the rituals and customs of *Rosh Hashanah* are serious, some are more lighthearted, but all of them inspire hope and a sense of rebirth and renewal. The Jewish year is welcomed and celebrated with candle lighting, prayer services, *shofar* blowing, festive meals following evening and daytime prayer services, eating sweet delicacies and other symbolic foods, and *Tashlich* service, the casting away of sins.

HAPPY HOLIDAYS

חַג שָׂמֵחַ

CANDLE LIGHTING
הַדְלָקַת נֵרוֹת

Had-la-kat Ne-rot

On the first night of Rosh Hashanah, it is customary to light candles no later than 18 minutes before sundown. On the second night, candles are lit after nightfall.

HAPPY HOLIDAYS

חַג שָׂמֵחַ

Holiday Prayers
תְּפִלּוֹת חַג

Te-fi-lot Chag

On both days of Rosh Hashanah, much of the time is spent in the synagogue, praying. The morning services are significantly longer than those of Shabbat or other holidays.

HAPPY HOLIDAYS

חֲג שָׂמֵח

SHOFAR BLOWING
תְּקִיעַת שׁוֹפָר
Te-ki-at Sho-far

There are many reasons for the ritual blowing of a shofar (ram's horn) on Rosh Hashanah, but everyone agrees the shofar sounds awaken the heart and remind all to repent and strive to do what is good and what is right.

HAPPY HOLIDAYS

חַג שָׂמֵחַ

The Shofar Sounds
קוֹלוֹת הַשּׁוֹפָר

Ko-lot Ha-sho-far

The rousing and unusual sound of
the *shofar* is like air raid siren for the
soul, waking those who hear it to
a higher purpose.
Maimonides, the great sage,
heard the shofar's message to say:
"Wake up you sleepers from your sleep
and you slumberers from your slumber!"

The sounds of the *shofar*:
Tekiah – One long blast
Shevraim – Three medium blasts
Teruah – Nine short staccato sounds
Tekiah Gedolah – One extra long note

HAPPY HOLIDAYS

חַג שָׂמֵחַ

THE SOUNDS OF THE SHOFAR

תְּקִיעָה

שְׁבָרִים

תְּרוּעָה

תְּקִיעָה גְּדוֹלָה

Tekiah

Shevarim

Teruah

Tekiah Gedola

HAPPY HOLIDAYS

חַג שָׂמֵחַ

Tashlich Services

תַּשְׁלִיךְ

Tash-lich

On the first day of Rosh Hashanah, before sunset, Jews proceed to a body of running water, where they symbolically cast off their sins. The Tashlich service is an ancient Jewish custom that began about 700 years ago.

HAPPY HOLIDAYS

חַג שָׂמֵחַ

Festive Meals
סְעוּדֹת חַג

Se-u-dot Chag

Festive meals are part and parcel of the Rosh Hashanah celebration. Honey and other sweet delicacies are included to symbolize the hope for a sweet new year.

HAPPY HOLIDAYS

חַג שָׂמֵחַ

SYMBOLIC DELICACIES

סִימָנִים

Si-ma-nim

Rosh Hashanah is filled with physical rituals that point at the spiritual world. The *shofar* blowing, the service of *Tashlich*, and the special symbolic activities during the festive meals.

The evening meal begins with the eating of symbolic delicacies that represent important prayers and hopes for the new year to be filled with joy, health, and prosperity. The holiday specialties include round *challahs*, apples dipped in honey, fish, pomegranate, a new seasonal fruit, and more.

HAPPY HOLIDAYS

חַג שָׂמֵחַ

ROUND CHALLAHS
חַלּוֹת עֲגֻלּוֹת

Cha-lot A-gu-lot

Rosh Hashanah challahs are sweet (some even baked with raisins) and round. They symbolize our wishes for a sweet new year with infinite blessings, much like the circle-shaped challah that has no beginning and no end.

HAPPY HOLIDAYS

חַג שָׂמֵחַ

Apple Dipped in Honey

תַּפּוּחַ בִּדְבַשׁ

Ta-pu-ach b'dvash

The nation of Israel is compared to the apple tree, the
most rare and beloved among the trees (Song of Songs).
That is why it is an apple we dip in honey to symbolize
the sweet year we hope God will grant us.

HAPPY HOLIDAYS

חַג שָׂמֵחַ

HEAD OF A FISH
רֹאשׁ שֶׁל דָּג

Rosh Shel Dag

Eating the head of fish during the festive meal
symbolizes a wish to be a head (leader) rather than a tail.
In addition, fish symbolizes fertility and abundance and, as
fish eyes are always open, it also represents knowledge.

HAPPY HOLIDAYS

חַג שָׂמֵחַ

POMEGRANATE

רִמּוֹן

Ri-mon

The pomegranate, one of the Seven Species of Israel, is said to have 613 seeds - the number of mitzvot (commandments) in the Torah. Eating the rimon and its many seeds symbolizes our wish to do lots of good deeds in the coming year.

HAPPY HOLIDAYS

חַג שָׂמֵחַ

New Fruit
פְּרִי חָדָשׁ

Pri Cha-dash

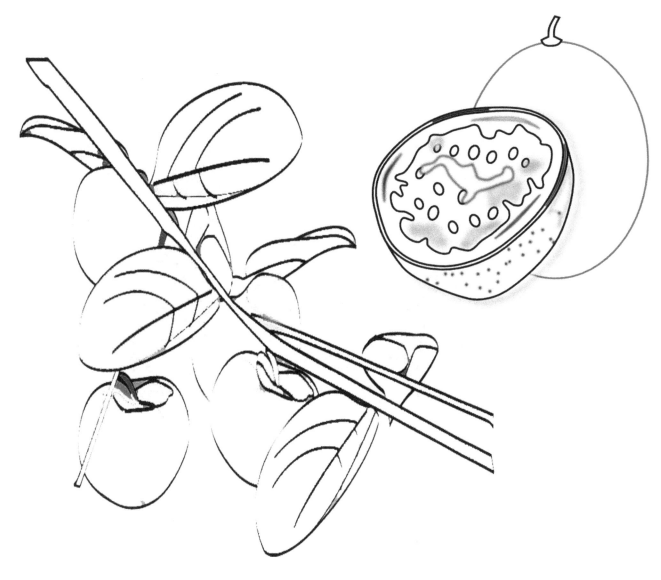

On the second day of Rosh Hashanah, it is traditional to enjoy a new fruit (an uncommon seasonal fruit that has not been yet consumed) to symbolize the newness of the year and add a special blessing, 'she'he-chi-ya-nu'.

HAPPY HOLIDAYS

חַג שָׂמֵחַ

Expression of Gratitude

We recite the famous *She-he-chi-ya-nu* blessing to expresses
our thanks to God for His benevolence and blessings.
We recite the *she-he-chi-ya-nu* blessing on special
occasions, such as:
- At the performance of a seasonal mitzvah
- When eating a seasonal fruit for the first time that season
- When enjoying purchases such as a new home or new clothes

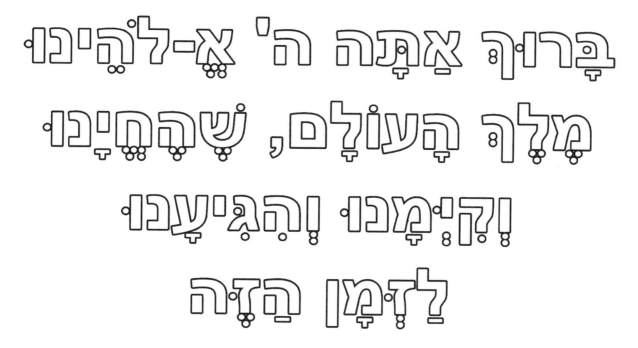

Ba-ruch A-tah A-do-noi E-loi-hei-nu Me-lech ha-o-lam
she-he-chi-ya-nu v'ki-ye-ma-nu vi-hi-gi-a-nu la-zman ha-zeh.

Translation:
Blessed are You, Lord our God, King of the Universe,
who has granted us life, sustained us, and
enabled us to reach this occasion.

HAPPY HOLIDAYS

חַג שָׂמֵחַ

Days of Awe

יָמִים נוֹרָאִים

Ya-mim No-ra-im

The Jewish High Holidays begin with *Rosh Hashanah* and end with Yom *Kippur*. Those ten days are also known as *Yamim Noraim* (ימים נוראים) – Days of Awe, and as *Aseret Yemei Teshuva* (עשרת ימי תשובה) – Ten Days of Repentance. On *Rosh Hashanah*, God judges us all and 'writes' in His 'books' the destiny that awaits each of us in the coming year. But, only on *Yom Kippur*, does God seal our fate. Thus, everyone is given the opportunity to improve their standing by repenting and engaging righteous and kind acts.

HAPPY HOLIDAYS

חַג שָׂמֵחַ

Yom Kippur
יוֹם כִּפּוּר

Yom Kippur, the holiest day of the Jewish year, literally means A *Day of Atonement.* It is a day for making amends, for apologizing, for asking for forgiveness, and for forgiving others. It is also the day that God seals our fate for the coming year.

The most famous *Yom Kippur* prayer is *Kol Nid-rei* (כל נדרי) – *'all the vows'.* The prayer is a formal cancellation of promises that we were unable to keep.

Ne-ila (נעילה) – *'locking'*, is the last prayer of *Yom Kippur, in which we ask God* to accept our heartfelt prayers.

HAPPY HOLIDAYS

חַג שָׂמֵחַ

THE VERDICT
גְּזַר הַדִּין

Gzar Ha-din

On Yom Kippur, as it is the day of final judgment,
Jews greet one another with 'Gmar Chatima Tova'
(גמר חתימה טובה) – 'May you be inscribed [in the
Book of Life] for Good'.

HAPPY HOLIDAYS

חַג שָׂמֵחַ

Rituals & Customs

טְקָסִים וּמִנְהָגִים

T'ka-sim U'min-ha-gim

Yom Kippur is a most solemn day, but it's also filled with hope that God will forgive all sins and grant us a happy year.

Yom Kippur traditions:

-*Ka-pa-rot, ritual of* symbolic atonement

-Blessings of the children

-*Se-u-dah Maf-se-ket, the* pre-fast meal

-Lighting candles

-Wearing non-leather shoes

-Fasting all day (bar/bat mitzvah age)

-Praying

-Hearing the end of the fast *shofar* blast

-Breaking the fast with a festive meal

HAPPY HOLIDAYS

חַג שָׂמֵחַ

THE KAPAROT CEREMONY

כַּפָּרוֹת

Ka-pa-rot

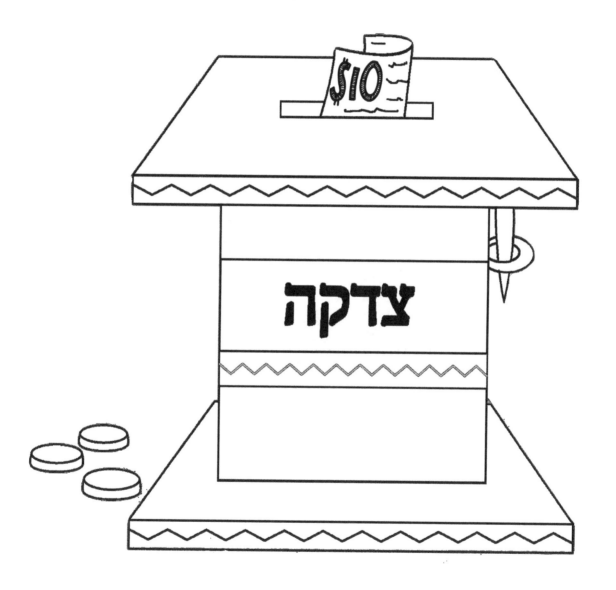

Kaparot, the ritual for atonement, is done with a chicken or money waved around our head three times. We ask of God that the chicken or the money (by the act of charity) cancel our sins, as the chicken or the money is then donated to the poor.

HAPPY HOLIDAYS

חַג שָׂמֵחַ

Blessing of the Children
בִּרְכַּת הַבָּנִים

Bir-kat Ha-ba-nim

On Yom Kippur eve, before going to the synagogue, it is customary for fathers to bless their children and say, "May God make you like Efrayim and Menashe [son] or Sarah, Rivkah, Rachel, and Leah [daughter]"

HAPPY HOLIDAYS

חַג שָׂמֵחַ

Fast Day
יוֹם צוֹם

Yom Tzom

On Yom Kippur, everyone, bar/bat mitzvah age and above, refrains from eating and drinking for 25 hours.

HAPPY HOLIDAYS

חַג שָׂמֵחַ

Yom Kippur Shoes

נַעֲלֵי יוֹם כִּפּוּר

Na-a-lei Yom Kippur

On Yom Kippur, we do not wear leather shoes, but rather, canvas shoes or shoes made of man-made material. Wearing leather shoes, eating, and drinking are some of the things that we deny ourselves in observance of the holiday.

HAPPY HOLIDAYS

חַג שָׂמֵחַ

Next Year in Jerusalem
לְשָׁנָה הַבָּאָה
בִּירוּשָׁלַיִם הַבְּנוּיָה

L'Shana Haba'ah B'Yerushalayim, 'Next year in Jerusalem,'
is a phrase that is sung at the end of the Ne'ila service,
the final prayer service on Yom Kippur.
This song is also sung at the end of the Passover Seder.

HAPPY HOLIDAYS

חַג שָׂמֵחַ

Sukkot
סֻכּוֹת

The joyous holiday of *Sukkot* follows the solemn *Yom Kippur* and is referred to as *Z'man Simchateinu* (זמן שמחתנו), the *Season of our Rejoicing*. *Sukkot* is the third of the *Shalosh Regalim*, the three pilgrimage festivals (when Jews gathered in Jerusalem for special celebrations of *Pesach* [Passover], *Shavuot*, and *Sukkot*). *Sukkot* (tabernacles) commemorates the forty-year period during which the children of Israel were wandering in the desert, living in temporary shelters. *Sukkot* is a harvest festival and is also known as *Chag Ha-Asif* (חג האסיף), the *Festival of Gathering*.

HAPPY HOLIDAYS

חַג שָׂמֵחַ

FESTIVAL OF TABERNACLES

בְּסֻכֹּת תֵּשְׁבוּ שִׁבְעַת יָמִים

Ba-su-kkot Tesh-vu Shi-va-at Ya-mim

Sukkot is also called Festival of Tabernacles (booths), as God instructed the Jewish people to build and live in booths. "You shall live in booths seven days. All citizens of Israel shall dwell in booths" (Leviticus 23:42).

HAPPY HOLIDAYS

חַג שָׂמֵחַ

THE FOUR SPECIES
אַרְבַּעַת הַמִּינִים

Ar-ba-at Ha-Mi-nim

The four species (ארבעת המינים) are four plants mentioned in the *Torah*, held together and waved in a special ceremony during the Jewish holiday of *Sukkot*. The waving of the Lulav set is a symbolic references to a Jew's service of God.

The Four Plants:

Lulav (לולב) - ripe fronds from a palm or date tree.

Etrog (אתרוג) - the fruit of a citron tree.

Hadas (הדס) - branches with leaves from a myrtle shrub.

Arava (ערבה) - branches with leaves from the willow tree.

HAPPY HOLIDAYS

חַג שָׂמֵחַ

Blessing the Lulav
עַל נְטִילַת לוּלָב

Al Ne-ti-lat Lu-lav

Performing the mitzvah of Lulav: Hold the Lulav, the Hadas, and the Arava in your right hand and the Etrog in your left. Say the blessing and wave all four species right and left, up and down, front and back.

HAPPY HOLIDAYS

חַג שָׂמֵחַ

Symbolism

סִמְלִיּוּת אַרְבַּעַת הַמִּינִים

Sim-li-yut Ar-ba-at Ha-mi-nim

To perform the mitzvah of the four species (ארבעת המינים), the palm, myrtle, and willow are bound together, with the citron held close. This symbolizes the the importance of unity.

Further, according to Jewish tradition, each of the four species represents a vital organ in our body. Every body part is crucial, but all parts must work together for the body to function properly. Here too the message is clear. We must engage with our entire being, physically and spiritually, when we celebrate *Sukkot* and perform the holiday's *mitzvot*.

HAPPY HOLIDAYS

חַג שָׂמֵחַ

DATE PALM TREE
עֵץ הַדֶּקֶל

Etz Ha-de-kel

The Lulav is a dried branch of a date palm tree.
The Lulav has a taste but no smell.
The Lulav, given its shape, is symbolic of a person's spine.

HAPPY HOLIDAYS

חַג שָׂמֵחַ

THE CITRON TREE
עֵץ הָאֶתְרוֹג

Etz Ha-et-rog

The Etrog is the citron fruit, which resembles a lemon and is native to Israel. The Etrog has a lovely aroma and a lovely taste. Given its shape, the Etrog is symbolic of the human heart.

HAPPY HOLIDAYS

חַג שָׂמֵחַ

THE MYRTLE SHRUB
שִׂיחַ הֲדַסִּים

Si-ach Ha-da-sim

The Hadasim (plural for Hadas) are three myrtle branches.
Myrtle branches have no taste but they have a lovely smell.
Given the shape of their leaves, the Hadasim symbolize
a person's eyes.

HAPPY HOLIDAYS

חַג שָׂמֵחַ

The Willow Tree
עֵץ הָעֲרָבָה

Etz Ha-A-ra-va

The Aravot (plural for Arava) attached to the Lulav are
two branches from a willow tree. They willow leaves have
neither scent nor taste. Given the mouth-like shape of their
leaves, the Aravot represent the lips (speech).

HAPPY HOLIDAYS

חַג שָׂמֵחַ

SHMINI ATZERET
SIMCHAT TORAH

שְׁמִינִי עֲצֶרֶת/שִׂמְחַת תּוֹרָה

The Jewish holiday of
Shmini Atzeret, Eighth Day of Assembly,
directly follows the seven-day holiday
of *Sukkot.* The most distinctive feature
of the holiday is the celebration of
Simchat Torah, rejoicing with the *Torah.*
In Israel, the observance and celebration
of *Shmini Atzeret* and *Simchat Torah*
are combined on a single day, and
the names are used interchangeably.
Outside of Israel, the celebration
of *Simchat Torah* is deferred to the
second day of the holiday.

HAPPY HOLIDAYS

חַג שָׂמֵחַ

The Five Books of Moses
חֲמִשָּׁה חֻמְשֵׁי תּוֹרָה

Cha-mi-sha Chum-shei To-rah

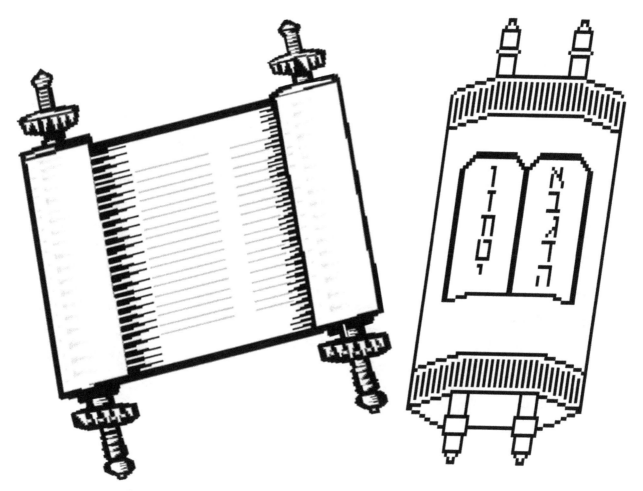

Bereshit בראשית - Shemot שמות - Vayikra ויקרא

Bəmidbar במדבר - Devarim דברים

The Torah, which is celebrated on Simchat Torah, literally means instruction and teaching. The Torah consists of the Five Books of Moses: Genesis, Exodus, Leviticus, Numbers, and Deuteronomy.

HAPPY HOLIDAYS

חַג שָׂמֵחַ

Dancing with the Torah
הַקָּפוֹת

Ha-ka-fot

Hakafot - circling or going around - describes a Jewish ritual in which people dance around the object or people celebrated. On Simchat Torah, we dance around the synagogue with the Torahs.

HAPPY HOLIDAYS

חַג שָׂמֵחַ

SIMCHAT TORAH FLAG
דֶּגֶל שִׂמְחַת תּוֹרָה

De-gel Sim-chat To-rah

Simchat Torah is a kid-friendly holiday. Children love to join the adults and dance the Hakafot. Some kids hold toy Torah Scrolls, but many kids dance holding a Simchat Torah flag.

HAPPY HOLIDAYS

חַג שָׂמֵחַ

The Jewish Holidays
in the Month of *Tishrei*
The Holidays in a Nutshell

Rosh Hashanah: The first of the four holidays, celebrates the creation of the world. It is also the day that our deeds during the past year are reviewed and judged.

Rosh Hashanah Observances:
1. Two-day holiday in Israel and the rest of the world
2. Candle lighting (both nights)
3. Festive meals with lots of sweet delicacies
4. Prayer services including hearing the Shofar
5. The *Tashlich* Service - casting away of sins
6. Refraining from work (like Shabbat)

The days between *Rosh Hashanah* and *Yom Kippur*, are called the "Days of Awe" and the "Ten Days of Repentance."

Yom Kippur: The holiest Jewish day of the year, the day on which God inscribes our fate.

Yom Kippur Observances:
1. One-day holiday in Israel and the rest of the world
2. *Kaparot* - the ritual for atonement
3. Blessing of the children
4. Candle Lighting
5. Festive meals before and after fast
6. Prayer services including hearing the Shofar
7. Abstaining from food and drink and wash or lotion bodies (Fasting observed by Jews above Bar and Bat Mitzvah age)
8. Refraining from work (like Shabbat)

HAPPY HOLIDAYS

חַג שָׂמֵחַ

Sukkot: A joyous seven-day holiday that celebrates the harvest and commemorates the Israelites' temporary homes in the Sinai Desert, after their exodus from Egypt.

Sukkot Observances:

1. A seven-day holiday
2. Candle Lighting on the first night in Israel and on the first two nights in the rest of the world
3. Festive meals
4. Eat (some also sleep) in a *Sukkah* all seven days
5. Perform the mitzvah of *Lulav (Etrog, Hadas, and Arava)*
6. Abstain from work (like on *Shabbat*) the first day in Israel and for the first two days in the rest of the world
7. The remaining days are called *Chol Ha-mo-ed*, which are semi-regular days, during which we still eat our meals in the *Sukkah* and continue to perform the *mitzvah* of Lulav

Shmini Atzeret/Simchat Torah: celebrates the completion of the *Torah* reading cycle. The cycle begins anew *Shabbat* after the holiday, with the first portion of *Genesis (Bereshit).*

Shmini Atzeret/Simchat Torah Observances:

1. One-day holiday in Israel and two-days everywhere else
2. Candle Lighting on the first night in Israel and on the first two nights in the rest of the world
3. Festive meals
4. Abstain from work (like on *Shabbat*) the first day in Israel and for the first two days in the rest of the world

HAPPY HOLIDAYS

חַג שָׂמֵחַ

Visit the Growing
MazorBooks Library

Children's Books
with Good Values

www.MazorBooks.com

www.mazorbooks.wordpress.com
www.facebook.com/mazorbooks
www.twitter.com/mazorbooks

MazorBooks Presents
Jewish Holidays for Children
Picture Books

High Holidays

Rosh Hashanah

Sukkot

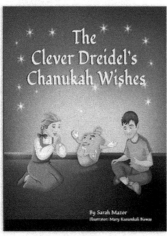

Chanukah

Purim

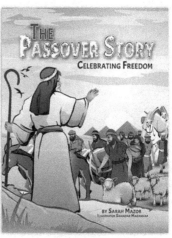

Passover

More Coming Soon
www.MazorBooks.com

MazorBooks Presents
A Taste of Hebrew
for English Speaking Kids

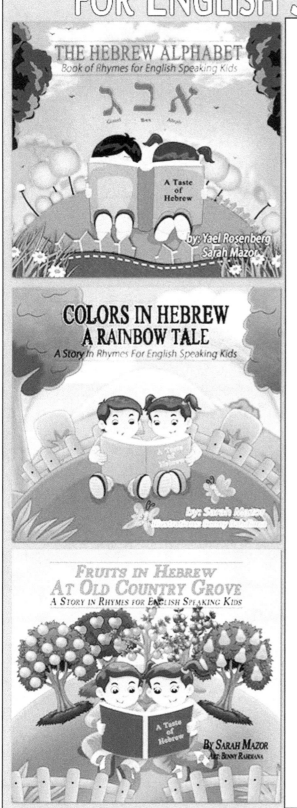

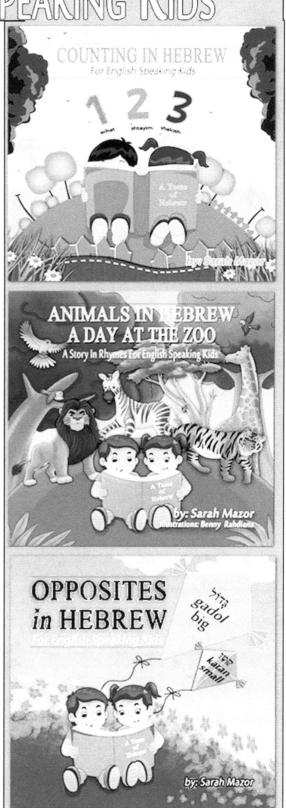

HAPPY HOLIDAYS

חֲג שָׂמֵחַ